## About AMERICAN HISTORY - A Veteran's Perspective, Volume I

What makes this book fascinating is that it discusses a selection of academic texts on American History by a combat veteran who speaks with the authority of someone who dedicated his life to defending this country.

Lieutenant Colonel McBrearty's reflections always maintain a personal perspective through photos and the selection of texts he examines. However, as we progress through the cultural changes and wars that shaped America's recent History, McBrearty speaks as a direct participant, and the book culminates in his poignant speech honoring his fallen comrades.

The book is truly a compelling and thought-provoking read!

From an Amazon 5-Star Review

# COMBAT ESSAYS

## *AMERICAN HISTORY*

## *A Veteran's Perspective*

### *Volume II*

by

## **John J. McBrearty**

Lieutenant Colonel, U.S. Army (Retired)

**This Book Is Dedicated To Our Fallen Comrades.**

*Five of the Armor Battalion's 1,000 Soldier's paid the highest price for freedom. Those Soldier's and their families are in our hearts and minds constantly and will never be forgotten. It is for them that I write this series of American History books. It is my hope to enlighten the public to what it takes to defend freedom and our way of life.*

*May we never forget our fallen comrades.*

*God bless.*

# Contents

# Contents

# COMBAT ESSAYS

## *AMERICAN HISTORY*

## *A Veteran's Perspective*

### *Volume II*

# Acknowledgments

I would like to thank the following individuals for their love, support, and encouragement. Without them, a combat deployment to Iraq would have been much more difficult: my wife Lynette, daughter Kristina (now Dr. Kristina Dhillon), son John Jr., Paul McKenna, Dave Dumond, Charles "Duke" Fleming, Chris Daiy, Rafael O'Bieta, the Gross family of Sacramento, and all the friends and relatives that wrote me and sent my unit greatly appreciated care packages.

Assisting me with the writing of this book includes the following:

John Cole, US Marine Corps Veteran of the Vietnam War and seven-times published author.

Ted Peterson, leader of the Loma Linda VA Writer's Workshop for Veterans, VA Strings Guitar Support Group, and VA Links Golfing Support Group.

Cindy Rinne, poet and fiber artist.

Bill Cushing, College Professor and proofreader.

The Veterans Administration, Loma Linda, CA.

Andreas Kossak (the book's editor and mentor extraordinaire!), founder of Written by Veterans and former adjunct professor at the California State University, San Bernardino, CA.

General Gustave "Gus" Perna, U.S. Army (Retired) served on active duty for 39 years; he was the 19th Commanding General of the United States Army Material Command and Co-Leader of Operation Warp Speed (coordination of the U.S. coronavirus vaccine response and distribution).

MAJ John J. McBrearty at the Tigris River, Iraq

# Introduction

The following is a series of essays that give a glimpse into an American soldier's perspective of American history. Upon the pre-deployment of the Armor Battalion, I was contacted by numerous local and national media outlets requesting information about the deployment. It was from these inquiries and the development of those relationships that I decided to send them updates throughout my deployment. We had little connectivity in the theater of operations, so telephone conversations were out. We were not permitted to participate in social media for security concerns. That left snail mail (USPS) and email. I decided to utilize both avenues. My method of choice was a series of essays. This book is the compilation of those essays covering a nearly two-year mobilization and combat deployment. It is my hope to shed some light for the public on just what it is like to be deployed into combat operations in Iraq (Operation Iraqi Freedom). It is also my intent to demonstrate how citizen soldiers, when asked to stand up and serve their state and country, can make a difference. Some names of the participants and units have been changed in an effort to respect their privacy.

God bless.

MAJ John J. McBrearty staging equipment in Kuwait in preparations for movement north into Iraq, 2004

# Chapter 1

## *A Day in the Life of an Armor Battalion Soldier*

2 May 04

It is already the second day of May, 2004. Where is the time going?

Our convoy just rolled up; excitement fills the air. CPT Cantez my Logistics Officer (S4) jumped up and grabbed his digital camera. He yells, "There here, there here." I jumped up too. We ran to greet the five-ton truck driven by SSG Canister (Logistics NCO) and CPT Morehead (Assistant S3 Operations Officer). The truck was filled with parcels and mail for our troops. I yelled, "This is just like the old stage coach days, the stage coach is here! The stage coach is here!" We all laughed and took pictures of the soldiers unloading their truck. There is discussion about the packages. Morehead says; "There are many packages for HHC this time, and CPT Cantez has four! Major, you have one too!" It was like Christmas. CPT Morehead went on to describe how our Chief Warrant Officer (CW2) Cliffs worked his magic and got his hands on many repair parts our unit. That is a big deal around here, re-supply and repair parts. Water for example; this place runs on water. We are fortunate to be in the agricultural area where we could utilize canals off of the Euphrates River. However, that water has flowed all the way through Iraq from Syria, and by the time it reaches us, it is hardly potable. We have a reverse osmosis water treatment unit here to clean our water. Without that, we have no water, and in 120 degree temperatures, you wouldn't last too long without it. So, this equipment needs to be serviced continually and parts need to be replaced. I can't stress enough the importance of our Chief and his abilities to get his hands on parts. He is an extremely valuable asset to us here.

Two Blackhawk helicopters just took off from our LZ (landing zone), probably a med-i-vac (medical evacuation). Those sounds are fairly common around here. Gunfire is also a common sound effect, particularly at night. I have told my wife Lynette that the setting here resembles that of the television show M*A*S*H or even some of the camps seen in movies like <u>The Green Berets</u> or <u>The Dirty Dozen</u>. It is amazing how similar <u>The</u>

<u>Green Berets</u> movie is to how we live and operate. Picture us in the camp that the characters of the film lived in. There are many similarities: tents, command posts, towers with guards, fence line, concertina wire, booby traps, local nationals working in the wire (in camp) by day and killing Americans by night, Soldiers going on patrols, check points, etc.

The last 24 to 36 hours have rendered no bloodshed from our camp or our area of responsibility (AOR). For that we are grateful. The mood today is joyous, particularly in light of receiving the mail run. Today I think everyone got something. Also, today is Sunday, and that might also have something to do with our light mood.

The temperature is heating up, hitting 100 degrees regularly. Weather in Iraq is based on extremes. When it is hot, it gets real hot, up to 120, but it felt like 130 or even 140 degrees! When the wind blows, the high velocity literally knocks down tents, and when it rains, it is a monsoon. The Iraqi people amaze me as they have weathered these storms for some 6,000 to 7,000 years. In fact, we are located several hours drive north of the City of Ur, which is said to be one of the oldest cities, if not the oldest city on the planet and the birthplace of the Profit Abraham.

As I mentioned earlier, today is Sunday, and I have a big adventure planned for this afternoon. At 1600 (4pm), the chapel has Catholic mass. The Catch-22 is that there aren't any priests here or anywhere near here. Our camp has one Protestant chaplain, and he is not comfortable doing a Catholic service for us and has asked me to help out as a Lay Leader, as he has several times before. I initially didn't jump on his request as I haven't really been trained for this. However, we have hit a crossroads; the Chaplain broke his tooth and has to be med-i-vac'ed out to get it pulled, leaving no one back here for mass. He asked me to help out with a non-Eucharist mass. I don't have a choice now. If I don't, the Catholic Soldiers will have no worship this week. So here I am with a Bible, pulling out the scripture, reading and planning some kind of sermon. I know my father, a former alter boy, would be happy and proud with this, and I will think of him each step of the way. I don't know all the rules of the Catholic Church and only hope I am not breaking any cardinal rules. Common sense tells me that some worship is better than none, particularly here. We won't have Holy Communion of course. In this environment, where death and mortality are a common denominator, soldiers tend to do a lot of soul searching and many find their faith.

Today I received several wonderful emails from my wife that contained recent pictures of our children: John Jr., age 2 years and 9 months, and Kristina, age 19. This really lifted my spirits today. Another way that I combat boredom, combat stress, etc., is by staying busy. I get up at 0600-0630 or so, mission pending, and often work until 2200 or 2300 (10-11 pm) in the evening. Much of my down time (if there is any such animal), I spend reading and writing. I also have been studying Iraqi culture and started an Arabic language class. Of course, if we have a night mission or an attack on our camp, any kind of schedule goes out the window!

Two days ago, I had a most rewarding experience after I went to the local village and met the local Sheikh, or tribal leader. I visited a school that we are rebuilding for the village. The villagers were most appreciative of our assistance and fed us a feast. It reminded me of Thanksgiving. It is customary for them to feed the senior guest first; they made me feel extremely welcome. A large part of our mission here is to assist the local communities with rebuilding. This school is a good example of that.

Some 97% of the Iraqi people practice the religion of Islam. Similar to Christianity's divide between Catholics and Protestants, Islam is also divided. For over a thousand years, the Sunni Muslims and the Shia Moslems, two factions of Islam, have had bitter struggles. We are most fortunate to be here in the Central Southern region where the populace is mostly made up of Shias instead of Sunnis. The Shias were quite oppressed during the Saddam Hussein reign and are more receptive to American intervention. The third large group of people in Iraq is the Kurds. They are mostly Shia Arabs and live primarily in the north.

Well, there you have it. This is a glimpse into my present day world. Not all of my correspondences will be this lengthy, but today I felt motivated to write in this manner. Fortunately, the words flowed. Yes, you can get writer's block, even in Iraq.

I have been approached by schools in the States who want to correspond with the front lines, and that is also keeping me busy. Yesterday I started building a slide show presentation of our travels. That will be a work in progress for quite some time.

I am also starting a charity drive for the local village people in which friends and relatives from the States send clothing and assistance here. Even simple things like tooth brush/paste, soap, pens and paper, and children's shoes or clothes are a luxury for many of the people here.

Until next time,

Major John J. McBrearty
Executive Officer
Armor Battalion
Central-South Region, Iraq

MAJ John J. McBrearty during services, CSC Scania

The Faith Chapel, CSC Scania, Iraq

Inside the Faith Chapel, CSC Scania, Iraq

Specialist Kevin Michael Halverson, May 13, 2004

# Chapter 2

## *Armor Battalion Medic Saves Soldier's Life in CSC Scania, Iraq*

May 13, 2004

It was just another day at CSC Scania for Specialist Kevin Michale Halverson, a highly motivated combat medic assigned to the Scout Platoon, Headquarters Company, Armor Battalion. "I had just come into the DFAC, where I joined fellow Scout Platoon members for a bite of dinner," stated SPC Halverson. He continues, "I no longer had my food set down when a guy yells out, 'He is choking, he is choking, does anyone know the Heimlich maneuver'?" Instincts kicked into action for this experienced Combat Medic.

"I do" replied Halverson as he kicked his adrenalin into overdrive. Halverson reflects, "Without hesitating, I just did it. I am a medic; you jump into action. That's what you do." SPC Halverson successfully executed the Heimlich maneuver, saving SGT Collins's life.

SPC Halverson, like so many other National Guard troops, is a true citizen soldier who received his call to arms on November 15, 2003 in support of Operation Iraqi Freedom II. Prior to mobilization, Mr. Halverson had been working as an emergency medical technician with the American Medical Response Company, for four years in the Banning area of Southern California. He lives there with his wife Francesca and 15-month-old daughter Brenna. Halverson met his wife Francesca while they were both attending Crafton Hills College.

By definition, the Heimlich maneuver is a series of under-the-diaphragm abdominal thrusts. It is recommended for helping a person who is choking on a foreign object such as food, water, or any other foreign-body airway obstruction. By compressing the diaphragm, air forces the obstruction to the air way. It is not recommended for choking babies under the age of one.

Dr. Henry Heimlich, M.D., ScD. is credited as the originator of the now famous Heimlich maneuver. Dr. Heimlich is also credited as having saved more lives in America due to the Heimlich maneuver than any other individual with the numbers exceeding 50,000 saved lives from choking and drowning. This procedure has been fully endorsed by the American Red Cross, the American Heart Association, and the American Medical Association.

Henry Heimlich, M.D., ScD., President of the Heimlich Institute
Inventor of Heimlich Maneuver, Cornell Alumnus
Image courtesy of the Library of Congress

Today, SPC Halverson is among those Americans who have saved a life utilizing Dr. Heimlich's proven method. When asked how it feels to save a human life, Halverson humbly replied, "It's not a big deal; it is my job." However you look at it, SPC Halverson has joined the hero ranks of our mighty Armor Battalion.

For further study about the Heimlich maneuver the following websites are recommended:

http://www.americanheart.org/presenter.jhtml?identifier=4605

http://www.nlm.nih.gov/medlineplus/ency/article/000047.htm

The University of Pennsylvania Health System

http://www.pennhealth.com/ency/article/000047.htm

18 years later, Lt. Colonel John J. McBrearty and Specialist Kevin Michael Halverson
meet again at the VA in 2023

Bahkan School Project before construction

Bahkan School Project after completion

# Chapter 3

## *Opening of the Bahkan School*

May 27, 2004

Wednesday, May 26, 2004, will forever stand as a significant event for our Armor Battalion as it participated in the re-opening dedication ceremony of the Bahkan Elementary School located in Southern Iraq. Attendees included Major Adam Strek, Chief of Staff of 1st Battle Group (from 1st Brigade Combat Team) MND CS (Polish Army); Major John J. McBrearty, Executive Officer of the Armor Battalion AR; and Muhamed Abas Jasum the Mayor of the Village of Bahkan—as well as a host of local villagers and eager students from the institution.

This school represents the opportunity for the children of the Bahkan Village to receive a solid educational foundation, which will have a positive impact on their future prosperity and quality of life. This project also represents the unity of effort with the coalition forces here in support of Operation Iraqi Freedom. This project was a joint effort with the Polish, American, and Iraqi people all working together for a common goal that has resulted in a positive impact on the community of Bahkan and surrounding villages. Once the project was funded, local contractors were hired to do the construction on the school. The result was "par excellence", stated Mayor Jasum.

On a blistering hot afternoon, the dedication ceremony was conducted at the entrance of the school. Mayor Jasum was flanked by Major McBrearty and Major Strek. Mayor Jasum cut the ribbon as Major McBrearty and Major Strek held it in place, signifying the unity of efforts in this worthwhile project. A large round of applause erupted following the cutting of the ribbon. The audience included American and Polish Soldiers, local villagers, and students.

John McBrearty, Mayor Muhammed Abas Jasum, and Maj. Strek of Poland, 2004

Following the ribbon cutting, the mayor and the two majors exchanged words. Through an interpreter, Mayor Jasum expressed his sincere gratitude to both the Poles and Americans for their gracious support of their community. Major McBrearty stated, "The future of Iraq will someday be in the hands of the children of this school, and we are very happy to have made a difference in their lives. This is one small step towards a prosperous future for the Iraqi people." Major Strek stated that he and his soldiers were also very happy to have assisted with the project as he handed out a multitude of soccer balls, basketballs, and footballs. The Iraqis served up soda pop and danishes to their American and Polish guests. Discussions consisted of the school and its amazing improvements and future projects for the area that could include road and drainage improvements as well as their mutual interest for peace. Mayor Jasum noted that this was finals week at the school, and Major McBrearty made light of the situation by stating, "Mayor Jasum, you have hit upon a universal nerve, the dreaded 'finals week' is equally discomforting for our American youth as it is for students all over the world." This was met with a room full of laughter as the atmosphere was joyous and celebratory.

This project is an example of how Iraqi people can work towards a better future. Local contractors were put to work to improve and expand this school and did a fine job. The project was a joint effort with Polish, American, and Iraqi people working together to affect a positive change. The school was identified as a primary school in need of renovation by the local Iraqi leadership. This need was brought to members of the 300th Area Support Group and the 2nd of the 505th Parachute Infantry Regiment (82nd Airborne Division) who contracted local contractors to refurbish and expand the school in the Bahkan Village. Later, the Armor Battalion supervised and inspected the completion of the project and assisted the Poles with settlement payment. This project not only improved the school but also employed 15 local Iraqis. The cost of the project totaled $50,729.00 dollars. Because the work was done locally, money went where it was needed most, into the community for which the project serves.

MAJ Mc Brearty with local leaders during Bahkan School construction

This is also a fine example of multinational efforts successfully coming together for the benefit of the Iraqi people as well as world order. First Lieutenant Romm Fernandez serves the Armor Battalion in the capacity of S5, Civil Affairs Officer and has become a significant part of the Battalion's mission in Iraq. He states, "This is great to see three different countries coming together in this community. If the Polish, the Americans, and the Iraqis can get together and build this school, the Iraqi people will learn from this experience and make Iraq a stronger nation."

The Bahkan School Project included fixing and beautifying the existing primary school as well as building four new rooms that would provide for a new intermediate school and an administrative office. Local contractors also installed new electrical wiring, fans, air conditioning, lighting, windows, doors, two drinking fountains, furnishings, and a new concrete pad with basketball hoops. With several hundred students in attendance, children attending the school are primarily from the villages of Bahkan, Boomkahlif, and Botran. Construction started in April 2004 and was completed on May 17th, 2004.

As the June 30th date for Iraqi sovereignty is rapidly approaching, the Bahkan school project is just a milestone for great things to come in the area of operations for the Armor Battalion. Working hand-in-hand with the local Iraqi civil and political leadership, this part of the Central Southern Iraq maintains a secure environment free from criminal retaliation, persecution, and intimidation. The Armor Battalion will continue to help the Iraqi people to build not only schools but a prosperous, secure, democratic nation where individual rights are protected.

Bahkan School Project – Classroom

Bahkan School Project – with school children and local Sheik

MAJ John J. McBrearty visits the Great Ziggurat of Ur.

MAJ John J. McBrearty and local man at the Great Ziggurat of Ur

# Chapter 4

## *Our Trip to the City of Ur*

23 June 2004

The thermometer reached a scorching 120 degrees Fahrenheit, so no one dared venture anywhere without their water bottle in hand as members of our higher headquarters (Brigade) and our Armor Battalion braved the sweltering weather to visit the Sumerian City of Ur, the ancient city of Mesopotamia. The ruins of the City of Ur are conveniently located adjacent to the Tallil Airfield in Southern Iraq. "Over here, its Abraham's house!" shouted Major Lukes, S4 (Logistics Officer) for the Brigade. SSG Canister (S4 NCO, Armor Battalion) followed as Major Lukes led 1LT Youngham (Medical Officer, Armor Battalion) to the rebuilt home of the profit Abraham. They along with other members of the brigade and battalion staff enjoyed a quick tour of the Ur ruins between logistical meetings at Cedar II and Tallil Airfield. Local Iraqi national Mr. Dhaif Muhsen served as conversant tour guide to this distinguished group of American soldiers. In perfect English, he told them, "I have been featured on CNN, The History Channel, and PBS."

Ur was the principal center of worship of the Sumerian moon God Nanna and his Babylonian equivalent, Sin. The massive ziggurat for this deity, one of the best preserved in Iraq, stands about 21 meters (about 70 feet) above the desert and dominates the flat countryside. The biblical name, Ur of the Chaldees, refers to the Chaldeans who settled in the area about 900 BC. The Book of Genesis (see 11:27-32) describes Ur as the starting point of the migration westward to Palestine of the family of Abraham about 1900 BC. Ur is believed by many to be the birthplace of the prophet Abraham.

The Mesopotamian City of Ur is famous for a multitude of reasons, among which it is presently one of the oldest cities ever inhabited in the world. Ages before the rise of the Egyptian, Greek, or Roman empires, it was here that the wheel was invented, and the first mathematical system developed. Here, the first poetry was written, notably the Epic of Gilganesh, a classic of ancient literature.

The first village settlement in and around Ur was founded (circa 4000 BC) by the so-called Ubaidian inhabitants of Sumer. Before 2800 BC, Ur became one of the most prosperous Sumerian city-states. The ruins of Ur were found and first excavated around 1854 or 1855 by the British and later by the University of Pennsylvania. In addition to excavating the ziggurat core, they partly uncovered the ziggurat of Nanna. The British Museum commenced excavations in the early 20th century here and at neighboring Tell. The expedition unearthed the entire temple area at Ur and parts of the residential and commercial quarters of the city. The most spectacular discovery was that of the Royal Cemetery, dating from about 2600 BC and containing art treasures of gold, silver, bronze, and precious stones.

Early cities such as Ur existed by 3500 BC. They were called temple towns because they were built around the temple (ziggurat) of the local god. The temples were eventually built up on towers called ziggurats (holy mountains), which had ramps or staircases winding up around the exterior. There the god visited Earth, and the priests climbed to its top to worship. Public buildings and marketplaces were built around these shrines. The temple towns later grew into city-states, which are considered the basis of the first true civilizations. At a time when only the most rudimentary forms of transportation and communication were available, the city-state was the most governable type of human settlement.

Of gargantuan proportions, the ziggurat mirrored that of an Egyptian pyramid. However it is now known that they were not burial chambers like the pyramids of Egypt, nor were they for human sacrifice like the Aztec pyramids of Mexico. Various theories have surfaced over the years that suggest that they were a nostalgic re-creation of the mountains the original settlers had left, an attempt to raise the city's god above the material life of the streets below, or even an attempt to reach closer to heaven.

The City of Ur is situated between the Tigris and Euphrates rivers. This area was known in ancient days as Mesopotamia (Greek for "between the rivers") where the lower reaches of this plain, beginning near the point where the two rivers nearly converge, was called Babylonia. Babylonia in turn encompassed two geographical areas—Akkad in the north and Sumer, the delta of this river system, in the south. All of the Sumerian cities were built beside rivers, either on the Tigris or Euphrates. The city rose, its brown brick walls held together with a black tar type of substance that is clearly visible today.

During Ur's supremacy (about 2150 to 2050 BC), Sumerian culture reached its highest development. Shortly thereafter, the cities lost their independence forever, and gradually the Sumerians completely disappeared as a people. Their language, however, lived on as *the* language of culture. Their writing, their business organization, their scientific knowledge, and their laws and mythology spread westward by the Babylonians and Assyrians.

Visiting the ruins of Ur and its enormous ziggurat was an arduous task for our Brigade and Armor Battalion staff members. Venturing through the ruins of Ur proved quite a challenge in the near-120-degree heat. "We had to climb down this long shaft to get into a burial site," remembers 1LT Youngham. No matter how you look at it, this hurried trip through the ruins of Ur, for the fortunate staff members of the Armor Battalion and Brigade Headquarters, will forever be recalled as the opportunity of a lifetime.

MAJ John J. McBrearty visits the Great Ziggurat of Ur.

MAJ John J. McBrearty visits with local leaders, 2004.

MAJ John J. McBrearty with Sheik Hatim, 2004

# Chapter 5

## *Letter to the Editor from the Front Lines (I)*

June 30, 2004

In a letter written by the Adjutant General to the Guard families, friends, and members, the general sends a well-versed message of sympathy for our two recently fallen heroes Second Lieutenant Andre Tyson and Specialist Patrick McCaffrey. The letter mentioned that, as of that date, the state has lost a total of seven soldiers as a result of conflict in Iraq: 25 seriously wounded and 75 with less serious wounds. The general's message was clear, to never forget our fallen comrades and to never forget why we serve: <u>to defend freedom</u>. The price for freedom is rising.

As much as I dislike being in the combat zone of Iraq in lieu of being with my loving family back home, I am proud to be involved in our nation's quest for the expansion of human rights and liberties. Having grown up in an environment that could be considered somewhat privileged, I have found that it is often commonplace to take our amenities and our rights for granted. After experiencing combat operations in this theater of war, I will forever be changed both as a man and as an American. I hope to return to America a better person and as a crusader for the improvement of the human condition for all citizens of this remarkable planet. If we are only on this great earth for a microcosm of time, I have learned that each and every moment of our time as well as each and every relationship is exceedingly valuable to the point of unfathomable proportions. Some Vietnam generational vernacular included "love the one you're with." After our experiences in Iraq, I have found that there is a lot of wisdom to that colloquialism. I would venture to say that for most, if not all of the National Guard soldiers currently deployed in Iraq have developed a new and enlightened respect and love for our country, our families, our friends.

Please keep the faith, and "keep the home fires burning."

Respectfully,

Major John J. McBrearty
Executive Officer
Armor Battalion
Central-South Region, Iraq

MAJ John J. McBrearty, convoy commander, headed north into Iraq from Kuwait. Notice the HMMWVs are not up-armored (covered with armor plating). That equipment came later in the war; these are vinyl doors and rooftops!

MAJ John J. McBrearty takes his convoy north on MSR (Main Supply Route) Tampa, Iraq, 2004.

Sam, Iraqi interpreter from New York, NY

# Chapter 6

## *It's a Small World*

12 July 04

Thousands and thousands of miles away from Staten Island, New York, a chance meeting at the small forward operating base Kalsu has changed the lives of two individuals, forever. For Specialist Robbie Catheter, age 30 from Moreno Valley, CA, a personnel specialist and member of A Co., Armor Battalion, a day in mid-April changed his outlook on his deployment in this foreign land.

The temperature that early afternoon in April was cooler than usual as the heat of the scorching summer had yet to arrive. Exiting the chow hall, SPC Catheter noticed one of the interpreters seated at some picnic tables was wearing a baseball jacket from New Dorp High School. SPC Catheter remembers, "My first impression, when I saw that jacket, well, it reminded me of home. My thoughts dove into my high school days—old friends, garage bands, playing my electric bass, the sounds of heavy metal music resonating from my bands garage, and of course, girls!"

After that moment of flashback pleasantries, SPC Catheter then realized that someone must have left this jacket behind, possibly as they were traveling through the FOB, or even a member of a previous unit assigned here.

2LT Larry Hong, 26, of Los Angeles, CA is the Intelligence Officer for A Co., Armor Battalion ant FOB KALSU. One of his collateral duties is that of supervising the interpreters for the FOB. SPC Catheter asked 2LT Hong if he knew anything about the interpreter wearing the high school baseball jacket. 2LT Hong stated that he was an American citizen who speaks fluent Arabic and lives in New York. The light came on for SPC Catheter as he deduced that this interpreter might be affiliated with his old school. SPC Catheter then met up with the interpreter in question.

After exchanging pleasantries, SPC Catheter discovered that interpreter Sam Nasir, 42 from New York, NY, was at New Dorp High

School in Queens, New York at the same timeframe in the late 1980's to early 1990's. Sam was the assistant high school baseball coach and SPC Catheter was a student at New Dorp. It turns out that Sam had coached many of SPC Catheter's close friends.

Catheter mentioned to Sam that A Co., Armor Battalion, was going to try and build a baseball field on their FOB KALSU and invited Sam to join them in the future to play some ball. Sam was elated by the idea.

For Sam, the momentary meeting also brought up many wonderful memories of his experience as a baseball coach. "It sure was good times back then; I never remembered a happier time in my life than coaching baseball," stated Sam.

Since their impromptu encounter, Catheter and Sam have developed a great relationship with a mutual foundation of New Dorp High School, Staten Island, New York. Together they have endured life together in Iraq at this small FOB in the Central Southern Iraq. From mortar attacks to civil affairs operations, these two individuals' paths crossed in a most unorthodox manner. Together they are part of the Armor Battalion's A Company and the results of their units work have been quite significant. The Armor Battalion's various FOB locations maintains an environment that is safe and free from combatants' illicit reprisals. The Armor Battalion will continue to help the Iraqi people to build not only schools but a flourishing environment that improves the human condition.

MAJ John J. McBrearty with local Mayor at a joint infrastructure improvement dedication

Local Iraqi with our favorite Chai Tea!

MSG Richard W. Casper

# Chapter 7

## MSG Richard W. Casper, a Life of Schooling Put to the Test

16 July 04

"I am now practicing what I have preached for the last eighteen-years!" states MSG Casper of his experiences serving in support of Operation Iraqi Freedom II. For nearly two decades, this senior non-commissioned officer has served the National Guard in a multitude of positions. Many of these positions were that of "school house" instructor. The various curricula mastered by this professional soldier include BNOC Instructor, ANOC Instructor, Small Group Instructors Course (SGI), Battle Focused Instructors Training Course, and Officer Candidate Instructor and Tactical Officer. The crowning achievement in his career was the completion of the arduous Master Gunner's School at Ft. Knox, KY.

This lifetime of training reached a demanding culmination point while the Battalion Armor Regiment (Infantry Provisional) was training at Ft. Lewis, WA. While the battalion was preparing for deployment to Iraq, MSG Casper was tasked as the NCOIC of the live fire range at Yakima Training Center (YTC), Yakima, WA. His responsibilities were multifaceted and included motorized gunnery, squad live fire exercises, and the conduct of seven ranges simultaneously. The Armor Battalion's Battalion Commander, Lieutenant Colonel (LTC) Larry J. Slacker, awarded MSG Casper with an Army Commendation Medal for his tenacious efforts at Yakima. "MSG Casper was vital to the combat readiness of the 1st-Armor Battalion," commented LTC Slacker.

For 18 of his over 26 years of military service, MSG Casper has served with the active Army or as a fulltime instructor with the National Guard. He resides in Palmdale, CA where he enjoys the solitude of living in a sparsely populated desert community, which he says is close enough to the big city for his liking. While on deployment, MSG Casper had the good fortune of marrying his wife Phyllis Casper during his leave in December 2003. Interestingly enough, he met Phyllis through his mother because Phyllis was her dental hygienist. One day a conversation ensued about

MSG Richard W. Casper. The rest is history. Military tradition continues in the Casper family as MSG Casper's son from a previous marriage recently joined the Air Force.

Duties at CSC Scania, Iraq for MSG Casper included serving as the Base Defense Operations Center (BDOC) Battle Captain NCOIC assigned to HHC, Armor Battalion. MSG Casper is currently on a leave of absence from his full-time position as an instructor for the Close Combat Tactical Trainer for the National Guard.

As for his time here in Iraq, MSG Casper reflects on his years of training and instruction; not only does he feel privileged to finally practice what he has been preaching (teaching) for years, he also is grateful to experience another culture firsthand and to help his fellow man/woman.

MSG Casper is among the 900-plus National Guardsmen and Women presently serving in Iraq. Most of those Soldiers belong to the Armor Battalion. The Armor Battalion's mission has its battalion spread out over various Forward Operating Bases (FOB) throughout Iraq. The Armor Battalion continues to ensure an operating environment guarded from hostilities largely due to an understanding of mutual respect and trust with its various local Iraqi populations. Forging these relationships has gone a long way for us to keep the peace in our various area of operations (AO). MSG Casper concluded that "a democratic Iraq looks quite promising."

MSG Richard W. Casper

CSC Scania, October 2004

CSC Scania DEFAC (Dining Facilities)

# Chapter 8

## *CSC Scania Gets Connected*

23 July 04

In an impromptu ceremony during a normally hectic day for CSC Scania Camp Commander, Colonel Quate Nosey dedicated the opening of the newly renovated MWR Internet Cafe. At 11:00 on July 23, 2004, Col Nosey, age 45 from Hacker Heights, TX, along with several members of the leadership of a Combat Support Battalion (Provisional) and our Armor Battalion attended an opening ceremony for the newly renovated Internet Cafe. As Col Nosey cut a yellow ribbon signifying the numerous recent advances to the many amenities of the camp, he reminded those present of the purpose of CSC Scania: "To support the soldiers in the field in order to assist facilitating Iraq's pursuit for a free and democratic nation."

First Lieutenant (1LT) J. D. Sonic, age 36 from Fontana, CA, is the S6 (Communications Officer) for the Armor Battalion and supervised the installation of 18 new personal computers as well as the expansion of the entire Internet Cafe. Sonic was assisted by SSG Brom Solan, age 37 from San Bernardino, CA and SFC Hank Thatcher, age 41 of Lompoc, CA as well as the contractor SPAWAR and other ITT technicians. Additional assistance was provided by Soldiers of the Armor Battalion.

Of the soldier's participation in the expansion efforts, the Armor Battalion's Command Sergeant Major, CSM Marcus Hunts, age 45 from Southern California, said, "This is a positive effort that all soldiers at Scania can benefit from." The commendable work done on the Internet Cafe improvements was done by this group of highly motivated soldiers in their off-duty time. Soldiers utilizing the internet cafe are allowed up to 30 minutes of computer or telephone time under crowded conditions and unlimited access if not crowded. "The new upgrades to the Internet Cafe make quite a difference because now you don't have to wait for big lines and don't have to be interrupted every 30 minutes," stated Captain (CPT) Gary Castellano, age 41 from Southern California, who is the Commander of Headquarters and Headquarters Company (HHC) of the Armor Battalion.

The Internet Cafe was previously outfitted with 18 M305CRV Gateway Laptops that were equipped with Intel Pentium IV Celeron 2.2GHz processors that have 128 Megabytes (MB) of Random Access Memory (RAM) and 20 Gigabytes (GB) of Hard Drive (HD). The cafe's upgrades include the addition of 18 Pentium IV 2.2 GHz Dell Dimension 2400 computers. These new computers are equipped with 256 MB RAM, 40 GB HD, a Logitech Webcam, and a Dell 15-inch Liquid Crystal Display (LCD) Screen. There are also eight Cisco IP (Internet Protocol) Phones, model 7905 series. 1LT Sonic stated that the increased RAM memory means that applications, or programs, will run faster resulting in more efficient operation. This will be of particular importance with the use of; webcams, instant messenger (IM), accessing websites, and other computer applications. 1LT Sonic says of the new webcams, "The webcam is great for morale because now families get to see their soldiers."

"Now, I can see my kids and family that I haven't seen in 7 months!" stated PFC Bobby Limmo, age 37 from Colechester, VT and member of a Field Artillery Company. Military Police Provisional co-occupied the FOB with the Armor Battalion.

PV2 Juan Caldera, age 19 from Pasadena, TX, is a member of an active-duty Army Infantry Division's Stryker Brigade Combat Team (SBCT) and had the honor of accompanying COL Nosey for the opening ceremony as he was the first soldier to utilize the new facility. Of the facility, PV2 Guerra stated, "Scania is a nice place, and I like the new facility." Also in attendance to the opening ceremony was SPC Jacob Henkins, age 21 from Farmington, MO, who is a member of A Co., Engineer Battalion. SPC Henkins, who works in the communication field in his civilian life, had the duty assignment at the Internet Cafe that day and was enthused about the expansion of the facility,

"Scania is a good post and this is some great equipment," stated SPC Henkins.

The expansion of Scania's Internet Cafe is yet another example of the "citizen soldier" bringing together a multitude of diverse backgrounds to their new assignments as fulltime soldiers. For example, 1LT Sonic is a data technician for MCI World Com, SFC Thatcher is a medic and full time Guardsman working for the National Guard's Counter Drug Program, and SSG Solan is an employee of the National Cemetery. The diverse backgrounds of these soldiers are what make Operation Iraqi Freedom different from any other American military conflict over the last five decades. Not since the Korean War has such an eclectic array of citizen soldiers been called to duty in a major combat campaign.

Interestingly enough, CSC Scania's Internet Cafe has had several official and unofficial names. The previous units that occupied the camp during Operation Iraqi Freedom I (OIF I) entitled it the Dragon Fighter Communications Center. Now that OIF II has brought new units to Scania, other titles have evolved: the MWR Internet Cafe, the Segovia Tent Internet Cafe, and the Segovia Tent. Whichever you call it, CSC Scania's new and improved internet cafe will provide countless hours of joyous entertainment for the tenant units of Scania as well as those soldiers just traveling through the Combat Support Center. COL Nosey summed things up: "Here at CSC Scania we want to provide all amenities to not only our soldiers permanently assigned to our camp but to those soldiers just passing through on a convoy. We are all soldiers in this fight together, and all soldiers deserve and will receive equal facilities at Scania."

The Internet Cafe's improvements are yet another example of our technological innovations that this generation has achieved, which has resulted in a better working environment for the soldiers who are serving their call to duty on foreign soil so very, very far from home.

BEFORE                    CURRENT

Examples of infrastructure improvements benefitting local Iraqis

# Chapter 9

## *Armor Battalion Makes a Local Difference*

10 Aug 04

The 29th of July, 2004 is yet another day that our Armor Battalion will record as a significant event in its regimental history. Elements of the Armor Battalion, along with local tribal leadership met at the access bridge to the Village of Al-Bahkan to dedicate the recently completed Civil Affairs projects in the area surrounding Combat Support Center (CSC) Scania, Iraq. These recent projects included the repair of the Access Bridge to the Village of Al-Bahkan, the cleaning of numerous sweet water canals of the Ibdaa-Gryaat River Basin, and the repair of 17 culverts along the Al-Bahkan Road. The significance of these projects was honored with a dedication ceremony on Thursday, July 29, 2004 at 1400. In attendance for this auspicious occasion from the Armor Battalion were Major (MAJ) John J. McBrearty, Battalion Executive Officer (BXO or XO); 1LT Romm Fernandez, Civil Affairs Officer (S5); 1SG Jeffery Silvers, NCOIC (Non-Commissioned Officer In Charge) S5 Section; and SGT B. Ferman, Project Engineer. Muhamed Abas Jasum is the mayor of Al Bhakan Village and also attended the ceremony representing the local population. Also in attendance was Salam Hussein Jasem, is a local contractor who represented the labor force that completed the access bridge reconstruction and other projects.

Completed civil affairs projects are mounting up for our Armor Battalion and the repair of the access bridge to the Village of Al-Bahkan serves as quite a milestone. This bridge serves as the main access route to the village of Al-Bahkan across the *Nahr Shakh* River and is the only way in and out of the village. Sections of the bridge had broken away and hung from the bridge, causing stress upon load-bearing elements of the bridge, which exposed reinforcing structures to corrosion. It was just a matter of time until this bridge failed entirely, possibly causing harm to local travelers. This project removed the broken sections, repaired the damaged areas of the bridge, and replaced the missing guard rails. Ali Abbas Jasoom, a local contractor, was selected for this project, and he hired local villagers as laborers, which brought greatly needed money into the local economy. The result of this project is a highly durable, ten-ton capacity bridge that will serve the public well. Whether it would be children traveling to school, local farmers taking their produce to market, or emergency services vehicles traveling to and from town, the new and improved accessible bridge adds to a greater quality of life for the local Iraqi residents in the vicinity of CSC Scania. Salam Husien, a local contractor, stated, "This Bridge and the culverts are better for the people of my village, and it makes me very happy." Amer Husien was one of the local laborers who worked on the culvert and bridge projects and had this to say: "This work is great for all the people here and we really appreciate it. Under Sadam Hussein's reign, he never fixed anything in our village; he only fixed up his own villages in the North."

Another recently completed project includes the cleaning of numerous sweet water canals of the Ibdaa-Gryaat River Basin. The Armor Battalion's Civil Affairs team identified the need of this particular community following multiple meetings with local tribal leadership. Their concerns were that the water canals were not free of obstructions and vegetation, which hindered flow for fresh water access. Removing the obstructions had a direct benefit to the local Iraqi populace as the clean sweet water canals are the primary source of fresh water for irrigation and raw domestic water consumption. By cleaning the canals, local farmers and villagers have access to more water during the dry season, thereby increasing local food production. A total of 14 villages comprising over 8,000 people and 9400 donams (23.5 square kilometers) will benefit from this project ("donams" or "dunams" is a geographical term used in the Middle Eastern countries). The result of cleaning sweet water canals is multifaceted; not only will the local farmers be able to prosper from growing more vegetables, but inter-village rivalries have all but been eliminated as water is now available unilaterally without conditions. The Armor Battalion's Project Engineer is SGT B. Ferman, age 37 from Los Angeles, CA and a civil engineer in his civilian career. SGT Ferman reflects, "The sweet water canals project allowed this area for the first time in many years to grow rice, resulting in a stimulated economy." Local laborers were hired for this project, again injecting money into the local economy. At the project's completion, the Armor Battalion's Civil Affairs team visited several of the canals clean-up sites, and they met numerous grateful local Iraqi villagers. Several children showed their appreciation by demonstrating their swimming abilities to the American soldiers, pointing out that prior to the canal cleaning, this feat would have been impossible. The local villagers now have the ability to utilize this free-flowing water not only for their economic gain from growing more crops but also can enjoy a better quality of life, as in this case, a swim in a clean canal on a blistering hot summer afternoon.

The Armor Battalion's third recently completed project was the repair of culverts along the Al-Bahkan Road. The purpose of this project was to repair 17 culverts that cross the Al-Bahkan road into the town of Ash-Shumali. The culverts were eroding due to poor initial construction. In some places, the road had narrowed to less than four meters. The direct benefit to Iraqi people includes safer and more secure roads to travel on. This route is the main road for three larger villages: Al-Boomkahlif, Al-Bahkan, and Al-Booternan, and their access to the nearest cities of Ash Shumali and Al-Hilla. This route is required for the transport of goods to market, the purchase of supplies, and emergency service access. Again, a local contractor and local residents were hired for this project, thus stimulating the local economy. The Armor Battalion's Civil Affairs Officer, 1LT Romm Fernandez, age 28 from Northridge, CA, stated, "Bridge, canal, and culvert projects like these will be left behind when the Americans and Coalition soldiers have gone, reminding the Iraqi citizens of our good relations with them."

These projects were high impact, infrastructure repairs serving the local residents immediate needs. Dollar for dollar, these were very high payoff endeavors as they had a direct impact on the day-to-day life of the local residents. Improving the roads and bridges has also added to the safety of our roving patrols that continually maneuver in this area.

To date, our Armor Battalion has been responsible for a total of just under $100,000.00 (US) worth of local projects. On the horizon are a multitude of projects that include the rebuilding of several schools and governmental buildings and improving water treatment facility capacities. The practice of utilizing local contractors and the hiring of local laborers for upcoming projects will also be continued since it improves the local economy as well as coalition relations with the local Iraqi populace.

Our Armor Battalion's formula for successful civil affairs operations has been threefold: 1) Identify a need from the local villagers. 2) Resource that identified need. 3) Oversight of the project's completion. These three projects are just a milestone for great things to come in the area of operations for the Armor Battalion. After thousands of hours of preparation, planning, meetings with local Iraqi leadership, guard duty, patrolling, interrogations, and arrests made by the Armor Battalion in and around its area of responsibility, the results have been profound. Working hand-in-hand with the local Iraqi civil and political leadership, this part of the Central Southern sector of Iraq remains protected against nefarious hostiles. Our Armor Battalion will continue to help the Iraqi people build not only culverts, bridges, and canals, but a flourishing existence for future generations.

On his initial visit to CSC Scania, the Brigade Commander, BG Kloster F. Kilman, had one clear message to the staff: "Make a difference. Make a difference for the betterment in the lives of these Iraqi people in your area. Leave this place next year a better place and a safer place than when you first got here." Our Armor Battalion is making a difference.

MAJ John J. McBrearty turns over joint bridge repair project to local leaders.

MAJ John J. McBrearty shakes hands with Iraqi police officers.

Foot Patrol in Central Southern Iraq

Detainees taken during patrol

# Chapter 10

## *On Patrol*

August 2, 2004

One word to sum up my day: exhausting! After a rushed workout with CSM Hunts and CPT Cantez, I wolfed down a hot breakfast at Scania's Dining Facility. By 08:30, I reported into the BDOC (Base Defense Operation Center) for an initial briefing and later went with the HHC (Headquarters & Headquarters Company) soldiers on a raid (a sudden attack by troops). I went in SSG Wally's vehicle and little did I know, this team was going to conduct this raid dismounted! What that means to a 44-year-old major who is primarily an Armor Officer (Tanker-Cavalry), is humping. Humping is what we call hoofing it or walking very long distances on patrol. Luckily, the weather was on our side, and it didn't break 110 to 115. However, the body armor, Kevlar, ammunition, weapons, etc., trust me, make for a very heavy load, probably over 60 pounds or so. I thought that this situation would lend itself to a unique video opportunity, so I lugged my DV camera along for the ride. So, there I am humping through the farmlands of the Central Southern sector of Iraq with all my gear, trying to keep up with the likes of 23-year-old SPC Halversen and SSG Wally, a former Infantry Instructor for the National Guard, and videotaping to boot! A camera in one hand and a loaded M16-A2 in the other, I must have been a sight, particularly trying to navigate over several man-made narrow bridges that were merely felled palm trees.

The purpose of the mission was to capture illegal traders in the area of close proximity to the camp. Yesterday there was an incident where one of these traders brandished a weapon at our soldiers and fired. Our Armor Battalion won't accept that type of behavior from the local nationals, and this was part of our response.

After what seemed to be a never-ending movement to contact, we heard on our radio that one of the fire teams adjacent to us apprehended two suspects. CPT Castellano was with a team that eventually linked up with our team as we all hoofed it back to the rally point. Unfortunately for us, Castellano and his mounted soldiers (riding in up-armored

HMMWVs), got their signals crossed and missed the link-up point. This meant that we had to hump back to the Main Supply Route (MSR). Man, it was far! And, man, was it hot! We were tired, hot, and sweating from head to toe. I did get some great video despite my challenges to keep up with the young citizen soldiers. We had to plow our way through several canals that were almost waist deep. When you step into one of these canals, you stir up the debris from the bottom, much like you would when stepping in the ocean, bay, or a river back at home. However, when you do that here, you smell centuries and centuries of smells, anything from sewage to dead animals to decaying crops. It is absolutely dreadful! I kidded with the other soldiers on the drive back that at lunch time, I was going to find LTC Milling and SGM Moan's table and sit with them so that my smelly, sweaty uniform would gross them out to no end. The troops got a big kick out of that. SSG Wally stated; "Yeah, that sergeant major is always hassling us about our uniforms; the mayor's cell doesn't understand that we sweat and get dirty in a war zone." (The mayor's cell is a small staff of logisticians who manage the day-to-day conveniences of the post such as living quarters-tents, latrines-bathrooms, and showers. They have been a continuous source of contention for our Armor Battalion soldiers. We are combat arms troopers rather than logisticians and don't always see things eye to eye with the "Loggies".)

When we returned to the base camp, I spotted CPT Castellano screaming at the top of his lungs at the detainees; he would have made Tony Soprano quite proud (the Captain is a native of the Bronx, New York and possesses a distinctive Italian accent); "I have told you traders to take your illegal crap out of my camp area! Where are you from? Ash Shumali? (A local town) Yes you are. You aren't from around here, and you better not come back and trade your junk in my area again! And I know that you understand English, so quit faking that you don't understand!" It was quite a scene as there were numerous soldiers dismounting themselves and their equipment off of their High Mobility Multipurpose Wheel Vehicles (HMMWV). An After-Action Review (AAR) ensued in which the leaders discussed good points and bad points of the operation. Overall, it was a success as no Americans were injured, and we detained two criminals. The interrogation of the prisoners was done with the use of Arabic speaking interpreters. After an interrogation session, we handed over the suspects to the local Iraqi police for processing.

Not every day is this exciting for me, but sometimes it can get a bit hairy. The weather is almost unbelievable, hitting in excess of 120 at times as we are just now getting into the hottest month of the year here. Words cannot describe how hot it is here. If you walk anywhere during the day, even just getting around the camp, you sweat through your clothes. Hydration is a way of life. It is sad to see local village children come up to you and not ask for candy or food, but for a bottle of water. Water is the most precious commodity here.

We are almost at the halfway point of our deployment, and I figure this is a good opportunity for reflection. I would have to say that despite the imminent threat that a combat zone brings, our service here has been quite a rewarding one. When we leave Iraq, our area of operations will be a better and safer place. We will leave this venerable community with many friendships and memories that could fill a book (now there is an idea!).

MAJ John J. McBrearty with contraband seized on patrol

Patrol preparations, CSC Scania, Iraq

Enemy action in Central Southern Iraq

# Chapter 11

## *Letter to the Editor from the Front Lines (II)*
## *My Worst Day in Iraq*

November 11, 2004

As I sat down to write this Veteran's Day message to the American citizens, I was interrupted by a telephone call from our Brigade Commanding General, Brigadier General (BG) Kloster F. Kilman. Our battalion commander is presently on leave, which makes me the acting commander and the one who has to take these kinds of calls from the generals. This was a call that I did not want to take. BG Kilman called to inform me that a Brigade Combat Team soldier that was recently killed by an improvised explosive device (IED) was one of ours. My heart skipped a beat. "What did you say sir, say again please...." I stated as the initial feelings of disbelief, shock, and grief set in. My emotions raced through my head as well as my heart too quickly to fathom. BG Kilman repeated his message, this time stating the soldier's name. This time my heart sank as he said the name as I vividly remembered this young man. Specialist Quoc Binh Tran, 26, from Mission Viejo, CA was killed at approximately 11:00, Sunday, November 7, 2004 from injuries sustained from a vehicle-borne IED that detonated near his convoy in Baghdad, Iraq. SPC Quoc Binh Tran was a member of Detachment 3, Company B of the Brigade's Support Battalion. Specialist Tran was on a re-supply mission for the Armor Battalion and traveling from the Balad area to CSC Scania, which is located in Central Southern Iraq, about ninety miles south of Baghdad.

The conversation continued on the topic at hand, as the general spelled out his command guidance regarding memorial ceremonies for our fallen soldier. With the current operations in Fallujah, the roads are too dangerous to travel so attending a memorial service at our brigade headquarters is out of the question. We will conduct our own service here at our FOB, and we will do the ceremony on Veterans Day in honor of this fine soldier who paid the ultimate price to be called an American.

Another one of our soldiers, SPC Dario M. Davalos, 20 from Tulare, CA, was seriously injured on August 14, 2004, while on a patrol near CSC Scania. He is currently recovering from his injuries and wants to return to the front lines. SPC Dario M. Davalos had this to say: "There are bad things about war, but war is war. Our country wouldn't be the way it is without people defending it. There wouldn't be anything to defend."

In the Veteran's Day Message from the Secretary of Veteran's Affairs, the Honorable Anthony J. Principi, the theme of his message focused on a poignant question "Have you thanked a Veteran today?" This Veterans Day is different for our generation as we are at war. Marines and soldiers are literally taking the streets of Fallujah as our beloved country celebrates this day for its Veterans. Over 48 million of our fellow citizens have earned the distinguished title, Veteran.

Dwight D. Eisenhower once said of Veteran's Day:

*"Let us solemnly remember the sacrifices of all those who fought so valiantly, on the seas, in the air, and on foreign shores, to preserve our heritage of freedom, and let us reconsecrate ourselves to the task of promoting an enduring peace so that their efforts shall not have been in vain."*

God works in mysterious ways sometimes. I can only think that, with the passing of SPC Quoc Binh Tran, SPC Daniel Paul Unger and the other soldiers that we have lost, God is sending us a message. To me, that message is to maintain my situational awareness at all times, particularly when traveling up north. It means maintaining that combat edge and not getting complacent. The Honorable Anthony J. Principi and former President Dwight D. Eisenhower both had similar messages to say about Veteran's Day: "Let's not allow our fallen Veteran's deaths be in vain."

Let's all do the right thing and watch out for your buddies and buckle down for the remaining few short months that we have here in theater. Let's all make it home in one piece, SPC Quoc Binh Tran would have wanted it that way.

To conclude:

The reality for our soldiers and their families on this Veteran's Day is that not all of us are coming back home. The price of freedom is once again rising.

Have you thanked a Veteran today? On this Veterans Day, thank them all.

God Bless,

Major John J. McBrearty
Executive Officer
Armor Battalion
Central-South Region, Iraq

120 mm Mortar fired

You are Cordially invited to attend a Traditional American Thanksgiving Feast to further develop understanding and celebrate the continued cooperation between our two great nations.

A Dinner consisting of Traditional American Thanksgiving favorites and Local Iraqi Cuisine will be served from 1330-1500 on 25 November 2004, at the CSC Scania Dining Facility.

Your host Major John McBrearty, Executive Officer of the Armor Battalion, would also like you to join him for Desserts, coffee and Socializing in the Post Chapel from 1545 until 1900 hours.

Please RSVP to 1LT Savage, Project Officer, not Later Than 1800 on the 24th of November.

HAPPY THANKSGIVING

• بسمنا أن ندعوكم لحضور مأدبة الغداء أحتفالاً بعيد الشكر على الطريقة التقليدية الامريكية من أجل زيادة وتطوير التفاهم ومن أجل الاحتفال بالتعاون المستمر بين أمتينا العريقتين.

• الغداء سوف يكون من الأكلات الامريكية التقليدية المفضلة ومن الطعام العراقي المحلي من الساعة الواحدة والنصف حتى الساعة الثالثة في يوم 25 / 11 / 2004 في مطعم جناح سكانيا بي.

• مضيفكم هو الرائد جون مكبير يدعوكم الخابط التنفيذي لوحدة 1 - 85، الجيش الامريكي ويحب أن يدعكم للانضمام اليه من أجل الحلويات، القهوة ومن أجل التعارف الاجتماعي مع الكنيسة المحضرة من الساعة الثالثة و خمسة وأربعين دقيقة وصولا الساعة السابعة.

Thanksgiving Celebration Announcement, 2004

# Chapter 12

## *Thanksgiving Day in Iraq*

November 25, 2004

To Americans, Thanksgiving Day is synonymous with being American. Thanksgiving is a quintessential holiday that Americans enjoy year after year. For the Armor Battalion, this year's Thanksgiving feast was not much different from those that have been celebrated at home with families and loved ones. On November 25, 2004, the Armor Battalion hosted a holiday feast at Convoy Support Center Scania, which is located in the Ash-Shumali District of the Babil Province in Iraq. The event included the company of many local Iraqi leadership: Sheik Muhy Bakhan Anad; Muhamed Abas Jasum, mayor of the Village of Bhakan; Lieutenant Colonel Ahmed Ajeel, Iraq Police Chief, City of Ash Shumali; Salam Hussein Jasem, a local tribal leader along with the Armor Battalion's LTC Slacker, CSM Hunts, MAJ McBrearty, Chaplain (MAJ) Farrell, 1LT Fernandez, CPT Ronham, CPT Miguel Obiero, CW2 Rolson, 1LT Ravage, SGT Herman, among others.

The atmosphere of this holiday event was based on camaraderie, friendship, and mutual respect. This was not a first-time meeting any of these Iraqi leaders and the Armor Battalion, and it won't be the last. The Armor Battalion opened up its festive doors to its local Iraqi leaders and made quite a favorable impression on them. Sheik Abas stated (through interpreters of course), "We are honored to have been invited here to join you in such a special holiday. It is like you have asked us into your homes as if we were part of your family." Sheik Abas and Police Chief Lieutenant Colonel Ahmed Ajeel in turned invited LTC Slacker and his staff to their homes for a future luncheon. The Armor Battalion's battalion commander, LTC Slacker, gladly accepted their gracious invitation.

This festive event was an opportunity to share the American custom of Thanksgiving with some local Iraqi leaders. Chaplain Farrell described to the visiting Iraqi's how the traditions of the Thanksgiving feast went back to the American colonial times when, in 1621, the first actual celebration occurred. The Iraqi guests seemed quite interested in the American traditions and had favorable comments about the cuisine. CW2 Rolson had discussions that included the bright future for Iraq, which includes freedom of religious practice, open public elections, and prosperity unilaterally available to all Iraqis.

Kellog, Brown, and Root served up a delicious holiday menu that included prime rib, turkey with gravy, mashed potatoes, sweet potatoes, stuffing, cranberry sauce, and pumpkin pie. The portions were plentiful, and of course holiday eggnog and sparkling cider were featured. Alcohol consumption by American forces in this combat zone is strictly against regulation.

The event took place at CSC Scania's stage, which is located outside of the DFAC's entrance. The weather could not have been better as it was a beautiful, clear and sunny day in the low 70's. The arid aroma along with palm trees flowing in a mild breeze added to the tranquil atmosphere of the day. The occasional distant sounds of KIOWA Warriors (Army helicopters) patrolling along the MSR served as a harsh dose of reality that not far outside the gates of Scania, a war lingers on.

As do many get-togethers of this nature, the topic of conversation turned towards the Iraqi leadership's desire for additional developmental projects in their area. Civil military operations have become a decisive operation for the Armor Battalion since arriving in Iraq in early April 2004. CPT Morehead, Civil Military Operations Officer in Charge (OIC), stated, "To date, the Task Force's civil affairs team has completed 36 humanitarian and civic assistance projects totaling some $270,889.00." By using the commander's emergency response program (CERP) funds, the Armor Battalion has been able to focus on the local populace's needs, which include five major areas: canals, roads and transportation, water systems, electrical systems, and schools.

Although minor in comparison to the scope of theater wide operations, this small celebration is just another milestone in nurturing a cooperative relationship between coalition forces and the local Iraqi populace. This celebration, as well as well-refined civil military operations of the Armor Battalion, has made a substantial difference for the Iraqi people in this area of the Babil Province.

MAJ John McBrearty, with local village Mayor and Iraqi Police Thanksgiving Day 2004

MAJ John McBrearty, with contractors at the CSC Dining Facility. 2004

Major McBrearty with Mayor and El Salvadorian Commander

Maj. McBrearty with Iraqi Police and El Salvadorian soldiers

# Chapter 13

## *Three Countries Working Together for Peace*

January 27, 2005

December 4, 2004 was not just another day for the Armor Battalion, who is presently finishing its tenth month of deployment in Iraq. I will remember December 4th as a day that symbolized the process that enabled three different countries with vastly different cultures that bonded together to work for peaceful solutions for Iraq's future. The newly renovated hospital in the City of Ash-Sumali, Iraq was dedicated at 11:15 that day. In attendance were the town's mayor, Amir Malik Hantoosh, Colonel Artiga (El Salvadorian Army), and Major John J. McBrearty (U.S. Army). As the mayor cut the ribbon, the two officers on his flanks held the ribbon in place, thus signifying the unity of effort of these three countries.

A large crowd of Iraqi medical staff, local Iraqi citizens, and el Salvadorian and American security forces were present and let out a thunderous round of applause upon the cutting of the ceremonial ribbon. Colonel Roberto Artiga Chicas and the unit known as Battalion Cuscatlan III El Savador Army Forces spearheaded the repair of the health center of the City of Ash Sumali, which is in the Ash-Shumali District of Iraq's Babil Province. The hospital is the only one of its kind in a city that hosts a population of some 10,000 Iraqi citizens.

Following the ribbon cutting ceremony, Iraqi medical staff escorted the three government officials on a tour of the newly renovated facility. An atmosphere existed that day reminiscent of a scene from a session of the United Nations General Assembly as no less than three translators facilitated communication between the Arabic, Spanish, and English speakers. During the tour, medical staff explained the uses of newly obtained medical equipment, which was also included in the renovation project.

The repairs to the health center included repairing ceilings and roofs, dividing a large hall into three smaller rooms resulting in a more efficient workspace, refinishing of exterior and interior walls, construction of a new fence, and repairs to numerous doors and windows as well as providing a myriad of new medical equipment. Commanders Emergency Response Program (CERP) Development Funds for Iraq (DFI) in the amount of $47,470 were used to resource the project. The Armor Battalion's S5 (Civil Affairs) team provided project management, oversight, and engineering assistance for the hospital renovation project. Once funded, the construction took 60 days to complete.

Civil military operations is nothing new for the Armor Battalion as its members have had much success by focusing their efforts in five major areas for reconstruction and development: canals, roads and transportation, water systems, electrical systems, and schools. The approach was three tiered: first, assess and identify the areas deficiencies and needs of the people; second, inspect, categorize, and prioritize the identified problem areas; third, resource the projects utilizing local nationals as contractors and work force, thus injecting money into the local economy. This uniquely simple and proven approach has been applauded from the higher military commands and could be considered a model for future efforts in Iraq.

The humanitarian efforts of the Armor Battalion as well as the el Salvadorians mark a triumph in the coalition's efforts to assist Iraq in creating a brighter future for their country. The grand reopening of the Ash-Sumali Health Center is a significant event here in Central Southern Iraq as it is yet another example of how three vastly differing cultures came together for a common cause: a better, safer, and freer Iraq for generations to come.

MAJ John J. McBrearty explains bridge building project to local Iraqi leadership.

Stryker vehicles are parked in CSC Scania's staging yard. These eight-wheeled armored personnel carriers are used by the U. S. Army and known for their great mobility and limited logistical requirements.

# Chapter 14

## *Letter to the Editor Returning from the Front Lines (III)*

February 22, 2005

I would like to take this opportunity to thank the staff at Grizzly Magazine for their support of our unit over the last year and a half of our deployment. Thanks to your support, our command message was able to achieve wide dissemination. The Armor Battalion succeeded in its mission in Iraq—to defend freedom. The Grizzly was there for us and assisted greatly in telling our story to the public.

The Armor Battalion made a difference in Iraq. Whether it was from improving Iraqi and coalition relations in our area of responsibility or creating greater hope for the local Iraqi people by providing jobs and opportunities, or even from the many rebuilt schools, improved water and energy sources, renovated roadways, bridges and other infrastructures to include Central Iraq's 1st American engineered and designed golf course that our battalion built, we left Iraq a better place. In total, the Armor Battalion executed more than 68 civil military projects in the Babil Province in the Ash-Schumali District of Central Southern, Iraq, spending over $844,700 of government funding that focused largely on transportation and utility systems. The results were profound, and the action significantly enhanced the local economy and promoted an environment of peace. The Armor Battalion also identified and justified an additional $1.2 million through a variety of government agencies. The Armor Battalion focused those efforts on areas that helped local residents stay peaceful and assisted them with rebuilding their own communities, thus improving their quality of life.

We had significant success in Iraq and have added quite a chapter to our nation's military history books. I wish to thank you for sharing our successes with your readership. Now that our battalion is returning from the Iraq Theater of Operations (ITO), we may now also enjoy your coverage of other units currently deployed throughout the world.

Your coverage of our fallen comrades is also quite noteworthy as it demonstrated the sincerity of our leadership's concern for our welfare. This coverage meant a lot to us in the field as well as for those family members of our fallen brethren.

Over the last year and a half, some of your readers included National Guardsmen/women serving on foreign shores. Your magazine provided a tremendous source of pride for the deployed soldier. By reading about their own successes in Iraq, the <u>Grizzly</u> enhanced the morale and welfare of our soldiers.

Keep up the good work of supporting the soldiers in the field, particularly those soldiers serving in harm's way.

God Bless.

Major John J. McBrearty
Executive Officer
Armor Battalion
Central-South Region, Iraq

MAJ John J. McBrearty with Sheik Hatim after an attack on our camp the previous day

An Armor Battalion Soldier overlooks one of many projects that made a difference.

# Chapter 15

## *Welcome Home Speech; Making a Difference*

*Paragraphs from "**COMBAT JOURNAL**, American History, A Veteran's Perspective," Volumes III & IV*

*15 Feb 05*

*Home coming day. I was so tired that several people told me that they didn't think that I was going to last through the ceremony. I could barely see straight and was suffering from extreme exhaustion....*

*We woke early, 0500 or so as our scheduled departure was for 0700. It took another hour or so to clear barracks and get manifests ready. C Co. was going to allow some 40 of their soldiers to drive home without our knowledge or permission. That was not going to fly as they briefed the previous day only six individuals needed POV authorization. I will deal with their leadership later....*

*We drove in five busses for hours to the Lake Arrowhead baseball stadium in San Bernardino. I led the battalion as we marched on to the field. The crowd roared with anticipation. Despite my exhaustion, anticipation and excitement rushed through my veins! I haven't seen my family for almost two-years, and now they were here, seated at the stadium. MG Ridley gave a very short welcome home speech and then it was my turn:*

Making a difference.

Honorable political representatives, MG Ridley, other general officers, and sergeants major, distinguished guests, family and friends, thank you for sharing this historical moment with the soldiers of the Armor Battalion.

In the military, our actions revolve around our unit's mission. For the Armor Battalion, our mission over the course of the last year was simple: to defend freedom.

The Armor Battalion MADE A DIFFERENCE in Iraq.

I want to take this opportunity to thank the soldiers of the Armor Battalion for their selfless service to their country. When their country called on them, they answered.

THEY made a difference in Iraq.

I would like to take a moment and thank our families for the wonderful support that they have shown us over the course of our deployment. "Challenging" hardly describes the environment that our families had to function in over this last year and a half. Our soldiers and their families faced many of the same challenges that our founding forefathers faced over 200 years ago at the conception of our beloved country. We have faced the same challenges that all Americans have endured over the years for the sake of standing up for and, if necessary, fighting for freedom and human rights. This time, it was our turn, and the Armor Battalion succeeded in its mission. And yes, it was a difficult road traveled.

MAKING A DIFFERENCE.

Whether it was from improving Iraqi and coalition relations in our area of responsibility, creating greater hope for the local Iraqi people, or even from the many rebuilt schools, improved water and energy sources, renovated roadways, bridges and other infrastructures to include Central Iraq's first American engineered and designed golf course that our battalion created, we left Iraq a better place.

The task force executed more than 68 civil military projects in the Babil Province in the Ash-Schumali District of Central Southern, Iraq, spending over $844,700.00 of government funding that focused largely on transportation and utility systems. The results were profound and significantly enhanced the local economy and promoted an environment of peace. The Armor Battalion also identified and justified an additional $1.2 million through a variety of government agencies. The Armor Battalion focused those efforts on areas that helped local residents stay peaceful, and assisted them with rebuilding their own communities, thus improving their quality of life.

## WE MADE A DIFFERENCE

I ask that each and every soldier's family members share in the pride that these accomplishments have brought to the battalion, to the United States Government, our State, the National Guard, and of course, the Iraqi people. By supporting us as you have, you all contributed to making these achievements a reality. Feel a great since of pride to be involved in our nation's quest for the expansion of human rights and liberties.

Each and every soldier who stands before you in this formation made significant contributions to the betterment of the Iraqi way of life. Whether they pulled guard duty in a tower or an entry control point, conducted roving combat patrols, or conducted civil affairs missions, each Armor Battalion soldier contributed to a common cause: freedom. In my eyes, each of these soldiers before you today are heroes.

As you all know, this success has come at the ultimate price, the loss of human life. Not all of us made it back alive, and we will not forget our brave fallen heroes. The quest for freedom has come at the ultimate price with the loss of five of our soldiers.

These soldiers and their families will forever be in our prayers. We will never forget our fallen comrades, and we must never forget why we serve— to defend freedom for our fellow man and woman.

This chapter of the history books is being written in the blood, sweat, and tears of not only our soldiers but with that of their families, friends, and communities. Without YOUR support, our unit could not succeed in its mission. Thank you from the bottom of our hearts for all your love and support.

After experiencing combat operations in this theater of war, I will forever be changed both as a man and as an American. I believe that I am returning to America a better person and a crusader for the improvement of the human condition for all citizens of this remarkable planet. If we are only on this great earth for a microcosm of time, I have learned that each and every moment *of* our time as well as each and every relationship is exceedingly valuable to the point of unfathomable proportions.

The combat veterans in front of you all MADE A DIFFERENCE. Each and every deployed Armor Battalion soldier is a hero in my eyes.

*(NOTE: DUE TO THE SEVERE ECHOING OF THE STADIUM'S PA SYSTEM AND THE FACT THAT THE SOLDIER'S WANTED TO SEE THEIR FAMILIES, I CHOSE TO CUT THE SPEECH SHORT AND ENDED HERE.)*

*To conclude, I will reflect on the question; What did I learn from this mobilization?*

*1. I learned how resilient the American citizen soldier is. Adapt and overcome became a way of life for us. When you can take a headquarters and headquarters company and make them an infantry company, and when you can take two armor companies and make them motorized infantry companies and succeed in your mission, that, my friends, is adapting and overcoming adversity. That is resilience. That is the Armor Battalion.*

*What else did I learn from this mobilization?*

*2. I learned how truly important my family is to me. I now cherish each and every moment with my family like I never knew before. The family dynamic has taken on a whole new meaning for me.*

*I also learned:*

*3. How so many things in my life I took for granted: fresh running water, paved streets, electricity, television, and most of all, living in a society where law and order is abided by. Living in an environment where you don't have to worry much about your family's safety. As the combat veterans in front of you today will attest, many Iraqi citizens do not have these amenities in their lives.*

*4. I have pondered the question as I am sure many of my fellow combat veterans have also pondered; what do I do now? DO I STAY IN THE NATIONAL GUARD OR DO I GET OUT? I believe that it is now our turn to continue to train our next generation of citizen soldiers so they will be better prepared in case our country calls on them in the future. This National Guardsman is staying in for the long haul.*

*As we journeyed through the difficult and often bumpy road of our deployment, I will always remember that the ultimate price was paid.*

*I will never forget our fallen comrades; we will never forget.*

*The Armor Battalion MADE A DIFFERENCE in Iraq.*

*I am proud to have served with such a distinguished bunch of professional citizen soldiers.*

*Thank you very much.*

*God bless you all.*

Grizzly Magazine on Executive Officer's desk in Iraq

# Chapter 16

## *Armor Battalion Mobilization Historical Information.*

1998 the Armor Battalion designated an enhanced battalion of an Enhanced Separate Brigade.

As a result of the September 11, 2001, terrorist attacks on our country, and the continuing global war on terrorism, the battalion was alerted for federal mobilization in support of Operation Iraqi Freedom; I in March of 2003. The battalion participated in a pre-Soldier Readiness Processing (SRP); however the unit was not activated from this alert.

September 2003, alerted for federal mobilization in support of Operation Iraqi Freedom, II.

15 November 2004: Armor Battalion activated for 545 days of federal service under Title 10 of the US code 12302. This was the first wartime mobilization of a combat arms maneuver battalion from the National Guard since the Korean War. Also, this was the first time the National Guard deployed armor (Abram's tanks) directly into decisive combat operations since the Korean War.

29 November 2004, Armor Battalion reported to Fort Lewis, WA for final Soldier Readiness Processing (SRP), which included processing personal issue items such as I.D. cards and cultural awareness briefings. The battalion also participated in pre-deployment theater specific training, security, support and stabilization operations. The battalion underwent three months of training at Ft. Lewis, which resulted in transitioning from an armor pure battalion to a motorized infantry task force consisting of both motorized infantry companies and a tank company. Training was validated by an active-duty Army Training Support Brigade.

February-March 2004: Armor Battalion participated in a Mission Rehearsal Exercise (MRX) in Rotation 04-04 at the National Training Center, Ft. Irwin, CA.

18 March 2004: the Armor Battalion arrived in Kuwait and started Reception, Staging and Onward Integration (RSOI) operations. The battalion would spend approximately 12 months of continuous combat operations in the Iraq Theater of Operations (ITO).

3-4 April 2004: the battalion road-marched north on MSR Tampa (the main north-south Iraqi highway) to its various FOB (Forward Operating Base) locations that were spread throughout Iraq from the Kuwait-Iraq border, to Combat Support Center (CSC) Cedar to CSC Scania to FOB Kalsu and LSA Anaconda (Logistical Support Area).

25 May 2004: the Armor Battalion lost first soldier, Specialist Daniel Paul Unger. (FOB Kalsu).

11 Sep 2004: MNC-I has recognized the service of MSCs and Separate Brigades currently in Theater. As such, the Brigade Commander is officially recognizing the awarding of the Shoulder Sleeve Insignia – Former Wartime Service (SSI-FWS) (also known as the right shoulder combat patch).

The Armor Battalion executed more than 68 civil military projects in the Babil Province in the Ash-Schumali District of Central Southern, Iraq, spending over $844,700 of government funding that focused largely on transportation and utility systems.

The Armor Battalion executed more than 2,500 combat patrols that included day and night mounted and dismounted patrols, raids, and cordon and search missions.

9 Feb 04: the Armor Battalion's first group of 300 soldiers departed ITO.

18 Feb 04: the Armor Battalion's first group of 300 soldiers completed demobilization operations.

12 May 05: end of federal mobilization order.

*Additional paragraphs from "**COMBAT JOURNAL**, American History, A Veteran's Perspective," Volumes III & IV:*

*22 Feb 2005 (out of sequence entry): Later in the week, MAJ Razi (our rear detachment officer in charge) mentioned that someone at the State's Adjutant General's office wanted a copy of my speech for historical records or something to that effect. I made him a copy on the 22nd of Feb.*

*15 Feb 2005: I didn't see my family until after the ceremony. I stared straight ahead in order to not get emotional. Lynette, Kristina, and John Jr. called my name, and I walked to them near the home plate seats. I couldn't believe how grown up my son had become. He was no longer in diapers and barely walking; now he has grown into a fully functional boy of four years old. No diapers and talking a mile-a-minute! I was gone a long time! I was so happy to see them all; words can't describe.*

*We made our way to a 2.5 ton Army cargo truck to get my carry-on bags and then walked to our car. We avoided the press as I saw this opportunity for the "Joes" (team of endearment for enlisted soldiers) to tell their story. Sure enough, that is what was printed in the papers, and I am glad. I have had more than my share of Armor Battalion stories published.*

*We then drove to the armory so I could get my bags. From there, we ate lunch at the Claim Jumper restaurant where we all enjoyed our last meal together. We even sat in the same seats that we sat in when Lynette's parents visited last. When we asked for the bill, the waitress said that it was already taken care of. I got a lump in my throat as I fought to hide my tears. I was in my desert camouflage utilities. and everyone in the restaurant knew what that meant (remember, this was February 2005 and our country was still in the post 9-11 shock). The management comp'd our meal. I was overwhelmed with gratitude. It took every ounce of energy to hold back a tear. I was so moved by this gesture. Truth be told, I get that same lump in my throat and tear up every time I read this paragraph. Some call it survivor's guilt.*

World Trade Center, New York, New York. -twilight view from harbor –Library of
Congress, Photo by Balthazar Korab
MAJ John J. McBrearty used this image as a backdrop when he informed the entire
battalion, of their imminent combat deployment.

# Chapter 17

## *Conclusion*

In summary, through my series of essays written in the combat zone of Operation Iraqi Freedom, I want to shed light on military operations in Iraq that are far less known to the general public. These operations include a multitude of civil-military efforts designed to make a difference for that country. While facing hostile enemy engagements, we built schools, hospitals, roadways, water canals, bridges, and even a golf course. These infrastructure improvements elevated the Iraqi citizens' quality of life. This book is a testament to how citizen-soldiers made a difference.

God Bless

# Appendix

## *Newspaper and Magazine Articles*

Quotes from

# *CALLAWAY GOLF*

Issue 6 / July 2005 / www.CALLAWAYGOLF.com

"One smaller chapter in the history books of this wary will include the creation of a no-cost-to-the-government golf course and golf complex. We called it, "Operation Iraqi Putting Green." Dedicated to the unit's first fallen comrade, the golf complex started with an Army Major's affection for the game of golf and his quest for the betterment of the Iraqi Citizen's condition."

"Golf in Iraq: this microcosm of American culture was widely accepted by the local Iraqi villagers. For the Soldiers, it brought a sense of hope as well as heartfelt memories of their lives back in the United States. For the Iraqis, it gave them a taste of American life, which they absolutely embraced!"

"For a guy who has only been in the sport for a few short years, who would have figured he would have had an impact on the game that spanned tens of thousands of miles, transcended multiple cultures, and even, in some small way, had a positive influence on a war?"

MAJ John J. McBrearty with Callaway Golf donations

Quotes from

# *Stars and Stripes*

## 10-9-2004

"Major's dream: A golf driving range in Iraq." "It's called Operation Iraqi Putting Green."

"Maj. John J. McBrearty, executive officer of an Armor Battalion, Army National Guard, is trying to bring a piece of American life to the wilds of Iraq: a driving range."

"By the time we leave here, we'll probably have a pretty nice golf complex."

MAJ McBrearty playing at the SPC Daniel P. Unger Memorial Golf Complex in Iraq

Quote from

# *Military Officer Magazine*

## *(Military Officers Association of America)*

July 2007 / www.MOAA.org

"Course of Dreams. – This golf course in Iraq is a lot like any other golf course—if you don't count the herds of goats, the machine gun nest, and the lookout towers."

MAJ John J. McBrearty with local construction crew who built the golf course

Local construction crew at work, earning wages to feed their families

Quotes from

# *News of Delaware County*

Article from 5-11-2005

"We are empowering their economy by rebuilding the infrastructure." McBrearty said during his lecture for the students at his High School and Middle School alma mater.

"We are helping these people, who really need help, by building roads, schools, hospitals, and water treatment facilities," said McBrearty.

"The driving range/golf course project took a year to complete-from its initial proposal through McBrearty's tenacity in getting the job done."

"When I left [for Iraq], my two-year-old was in diapers and talking in single words. By the time I came back, he was potty trained and speaking in full sentences... I lost two years of my life."

"Getting stability into that region is our strategic interest" said McBrearty.

A curious camel visits the golf course.

*Additional paragraph from "***COMBAT JOURNAL***, *American History, A Veteran's Perspective," Volumes III & IV.*

### *Email from my daughter Kristina:*

*17 May 2005*

Hey dad,

That story about your golf course in Iraq was really cool! I think it's cool how you haven't even been playing golf for that long and don't compete and yet you still seem to make your way into the golfing press. Many people play golf for years and years and never once get their name so much as listed in a piece of published text. Pretty cool stuff!! The media seems to love you!

Love,
Kristina

Kristina and John McBrearty at the 2011 Toyota Grand Prix
of Long Beach. My daughter was selected as Miss Inland
Empire for the Miss California competition.

# A Positive Change

The 1/185th Armor Regiment helps renovate a school in Iraq.

Major John J. McBrearty (left) and Major Adam Strek (2nd from right with sunglasses) perform the ribbon cutting honors with Mayor Muhamed Abas Jasum.

**By Major John J. McBrearty**
**1/185th Armor Regiment**

Wednesday May 26, 2004 will forever be earmarked as a significant event for the First Battalion, 185th Armor Regiment, 81st Brigade Combat Team, as it participated in the re-opening dedication ceremony of the Bahkan Elementary School, located in Southern Iraq. Attendees included Major Adam Strek, Chief of Staff of 1st Battle Group (from 1st Brigade Combat Team) MND CS (Polish Army); Major John J. McBrearty, Executive Officer of the 1-185th Armor; and Muhamed Abas Jasum, the Mayor of the Village of Bahkan, as well as a host of local villagers and eager students from the institution.

The school represents the opportunity for the children of the Bahkan Village to receive a solid educational foundation that will have a positive impact on their future prosperity and quality of life. The project also represents the unity of effort with the coalition forces in the area in support of Operation IRAQI FREEDOM. The project was a joint effort with the Polish, American, and Iraqi people all working together for a common goal that has resulted in a positive impact on the community of Bahkan and surrounding villages. Once the project was funded, local contractors were hired to do the construction on the school. The result was "par excellence," stated Mayor Jasum.

On a blistering hot afternoon, the dedication ceremony was conducted at the entrance of the school. Mayor Jasum cut the ribbon as Major McBrearty and Major Strek held it in place, signifying the unity of efforts in this worthwhile project. Major McBrearty stated, "The future of Iraq will someday be in the hands of the children of this school, and we are very happy to have made a difference in their lives. This is one small step towards a prosperous future for the Iraqi people."

This project is an example of how Iraqi people can work towards a better future. Local contractors were put to work to improve and expand this school and did a fine job. The school was identified as a primary school in need of renovation by the local Iraqi leadership.

This is also a fine example of the multinational efforts successfully coming together for the benefit for the Iraqi people as well as world order. First Lieutenant Thomas Hernandez serves the 185th in the capacity of S5, Civil Affairs Officer, and has become a significant part of the Battalion's mission in Iraq. He states, "This is great to see three different countries coming together in this community. If the Polish, the American's, and the Iraqi's can get together and build this school, the Iraqi people will learn from this experience and make Iraq a stronger nation."

The Bahkan School Project included, fixing and beautifying the existing primary school, as well as building four new rooms that would provide for a new intermediate school and an administrative office. Local contractors also installed, new electrical wiring, fans, air conditioning, lighting, windows, doors, two drinking fountains, furnishings, and a new concrete pad and basketball hoops. With several hundred students in attendance, children attending the school are primarily from the Villages of Bahkan, Boomkahlif and Botran. Construction started in April 2004 and was completed on May 17th, 2004

The Bahkan school project is just a milestone for great things to come in the area of operations for the 185th. Working hand-in-hand with the local Iraqi civil and political leadership, this part of Southern Iraq maintains a secure environment free from criminal retaliation, persecution and intimidation. The 185th will continue to help the Iraqi people to build not only schools, but a prosperous, secure, democratic nation where individual rights are protected. 🐾

*NOTE: 1Lt. Thomas Hernandez, S5, 1-185 Armor, contributed to this story.*

Major John McBrearty poses with local villagers in front of the schoolhouse during renovation.

The Iraqi school house renovation was completed just in time for final exam week.

# Guard hangs tough despite attacks

**IRAQ:** One soldier in the San Bernardino unit died and 10 others were injured in mortar assault.

BY JOHN F. BERRY
THE PRESS-ENTERPRISE

The May 25 mortar attacks that killed one soldier and wounded 10 others from a San Bernardino-based National Guard unit in Iraq was a reminder of the reality of war, its second-in-command said Tuesday.

"The death of a soldier hit us really hard," said Maj. John McBrearty, executive officer of the 1st Battalion, 185th Armor Regiment.

McBrearty, in an interview from his location south of Baghdad, discussed how his California Army National Guard unit has dealt with mortars, mission, Iraqis and life since reaching

Maj. John McBrearty, left, is shown with Sheikh Hatim Al Jarian.

the Middle East in March.

Spc. David Paul Unger, 19, of Exeter was killed and 10 other soldiers were wounded in mortar attacks on different unit locations on May 25, McBrearty said. Unger was the battalion's first soldier to be killed in action.

"It caused all of us to do some reflection," McBrearty said. "It heightened our sense of awareness of our surroundings."

Lt. Col. Doug Hart, spokesman for the California National Guard, said Tuesday that Unger is the fifth California Army National Guard soldier killed in action. Information about soldiers wounded in action is not released, he said.

Despite the mortar attacks, McBrearty stressed that battalion commander Lt. Col. James Sayers does not want family members to worry. The unit underwent realistic training at Fort Irwin before leaving for the Middle East.

"We're on par with any active-duty unit, bar none," said McBrearty, a Riverside resident.

Marlene Juchartz of San Bernardino

PLEASE SEE **GUARD, B6A**

## GUARD

CONTINUED FROM **B1**

nardino said Tuesday that she talks with her son, Spc. Eric Juchartz, once a week and exchanges e-mail with him. The 20-year-old medic is doing well, she said, but she cannot stop worrying about him.

"He told me, 'Mom, don't listen to the news.' But I can't help it," she said. "I don't think anybody in that country is safe."

Marlene Juchartz said her son often works with civilians. That is part of a coalition effort to help the Iraqis transition to democracy, said Marine Capt. Bruce Frame, a spokesman with Central Command at MacDill Air Force Base, Fla.

Figures from Central Command, responsible for the Middle East, show that the United States has dedicated $20 billion to reconstruction and development efforts in Iraq. That includes immunizing 5 million children, improving electricity to levels exceeding pre-invasion figures and rehabilitating 2,500 schools.

McBrearty said unit soldiers patrol around the clock, but most of the unit's work focuses on humanitarian-assistance projects ranging from medical care and water filtration to road projects and school renovation. He said the unit has a positive relationship with local Shiite leaders.

"We work hand-in-hand with the locals," he said. "If a bad guy comes in the area, they will tip us off."

McBrearty said the morale among soldiers is high. They have access to phones and the Internet, he said. The soldiers live in groups of up to a dozen in air-conditioned tents. Outside temperatures can reach 120 degrees.

The battalion is spread among four locations, three south of Baghdad and one north of the city, he said. Security concerns prevent him from being more specific.

The unit, according to a press release, is equipped with armored Humvees that have reinforced steel-plating, bulletproof windshields and machine guns or grenade launchers.

McBrearty said soldiers must contend with ambushes, car bombs and mortar attacks, but the unit's experiences are not as intense as the images Americans see on television.

"We are so far removed from Abu Ghraib," McBrearty said, referring to the prisoner-abuse scandal. "It's a different world

from us."

The soldiers are aware that the Army might keep them in Iraq longer than their initial one-year tour, he said.

"It's eight to nine months away. We will cross that bridge when we get to it," he said of a possible extension. "At this point, all of us will accept our fate. There isn't much we can do about it."

McBrearty's battalion of more than 750 citizen-soldiers normally is headquartered near downtown San Bernardino. The battalion was called to active duty last year and merged into the 81st Separate Armor Brigade with the Washington Army National Guard.

Hart said nearly 1,900 California Army Guard soldiers, and more than 450 Guard airmen, are mobilized for federal service and spread across the globe. About 900 California Army Guard soldiers are in Iraq, he said

More of the state's 21,000 Guard members could soon be called to active duty, he said. Individual units have not yet been selected.

"There are a number (of units) on the horizon," Hart said. "We're going to be looking at a pretty large number."

*Reach John F. Berry at (909) 806-3058 or jberry@pe.com*

MAJ John J. McBrearty in the city of Hilla, Iraq, 2004

# From the Desk of
# Major John J. McBrearty

*TO: High School Class of 1978*

*SUBJECT: LIFE*

*DATE: May 19, 2004*

**Dear Fellow Alumni,**

The responses to Peggy's email have been overwhelming. I am not in a position to email everyone, so I came up with the idea of a concentrated effort. This is a response to the many alumni that did email or write me. Many expressed their support and concern for our well-being overseas. Thank you all very much, and please say a prayer for my men and women.

# A FRIEND

It is funny; the last letter that I wrote was to my "very best friend in my whole world" hopefully, we all have someone that we can trust and enjoy the benefits of such a relationship with as I have with my Marine Corps buddy, Duke. Duke and I went together through NROTC U. S. Marine Corps OCS at Quantico, VA, many years ago and have always remained close friends. Friendship, have you experienced true friendship? Friendship, to me, is trust. Trusting someone with what is important to you; your home, your life, the life of your spouse, or the ultimate, the life of your child: THAT IS A FRIEND! A TRUE FRIEND! If you have had the pleasure in life to experience this phenomenon, embrace it as you are truly blessed. If you have not, pursue it because that is WHAT LIFE IS ALL ABOUT. The reason why I bring up the point of my friend Duke is that the letter that I wrote him gave him guidance on how to handle my business and personal affairs if I don't make it back home. No one here wants that to happen to any of us, and we do everything in our power to prevent it, but war is war, and things happen. You never know. This is my reality.

# EGO

To some degree or another, we all have one. Some EGOs are bigger than others. Folks, there isn't time for EGO where I am right now. I have seen people get killed because of EGOs, and that is tragic. My motive for writing you after all these years, or for writing a book for that matter, is not EGO based. I could care less what people think of me; again, there is no time for that. I guess at the age of 44, what I find important to me now is what my three-year-old boy might think of his father in the event that he doesn't make it home from his combat mission. I also think of how I would be remembered by my nineteen-year-old college student daughter, Kristina. (Is a proud father tooting his horn? You bet your ass he is! I love my daughter so much; she means more to me than life itself!) I am so proud of Kristina. She is going to make a superb Physician. I often wonder, "Did I spend enough time with her as she grew up?" Little John Jr. could just be the next TIGER WOODS. Look for his name in "Golf Digest" magazine someday because I bought his first set of golf clubs when he was 8 months old! At age 2 he could swing and hit the ball. Moreover, at age 3, he is dangerous, yes, dangerously good at hitting a golf ball with a golf club.

# MY LIFE

When we graduated High School, I spent "Senior Week" like many of you in Ocean City and Margate, New Jersey (yes, I know that I just "grabbed my audience" because if you don't have a memory from that experience, well, you must have been living under a rock back then!) When we left high school, and when senior week was over, I went to Ft. Knox, KY, for Reserve Officer Training Corps (Army ROTC) Basic Camp in preparation for my Plebe year at Valley Forge Military Academy and College (VFMA & C). I enlisted into the United States Marine Corps Reserve (USMCR) the following summer. Although I was already in college and in good standing to become a Commissioned Officer in the military, I felt that it was important to start my military career from the very bottom; a Private in the USMC. I have absolutely no regrets about that decision. In later years as an officer, I sensed that the enlisted troops that you led actually showed you greater respect than the other officers because I was once one of them, formerly enlisted. I digress; after another year at VFMA & C and my USMCR affiliation, I transferred to Temple University and pursued a degree in Communications. I participated in Villanova University's NROTC program and received a commission as Officer of Marines upon my graduation from Temple in August of 1982. Following college, I served on active duty with the Marine Corps. While at Temple, I met my lovely wife, Lynette. We had our firstborn one year after our marriage (a novel concept these days, marriage before childbirth?) (Excuse my cynical commentary, hell, I am 44 like many of you and have earned the right to bitch about things from time to time!)

After my hitch with the Marine Corps, I threw myself into theater study with world-renowned thespians Sanford Meissner, Bob Carnegie, and Jeff Goldblum. I eventually got my Screen Actors Guild card, but I never really landed any big parts in Hollywood. The first role that I auditioned for was that of a Marine Corps 1st Lieutenant. No joke. My previous work history was that of an active-duty Marine Corps 1st Lieutenant! Needless to say, the Hollywood dimwits of that particular project didn't think that I was the right guy for that role????? WTF! That, my friends, is how Hollywood works. Good luck with that life! Not for me. I wanted to be a rock-steady provider for my family and raise my kids in a good neighborhood. Hollywood was not that answer and was certainly not a neighborhood to raise a family that I was comfortable with.

Eventually, my calling for the military life drew me back in, and I was once again reacquainted with the military via the National Guard. I found one of the best-kept secrets in the military; the Active Guard Reserve (AGR) program. As an AGR, you serve on active duty with all of the appropriate benefits of active-duty military, all the while working within your home state. Through a series of assignments, I landed the position as Executive Officer of an Armor Battalion. This battalion is an enhanced Armor Battalion and is assigned to one of only fifteen enhanced brigades in the U.S. Army. The enhanced brigades are better equipped and better trained than the regular Nation Guard and Reserves. If the Active

Component Army is in need of additional forces, such as in a wartime situation, they first utilize the enhanced brigades. What are the consequences of being a member of an enhanced brigade? Deployment to Iraq in support of Operation Iraqi Freedom. A philosophy that Sanford Meisner stressed in his teachings to his younger students was to *experience life*. He said go out and live your life for 20 years and then come back to me, and you will be ready to become an actor or filmmaker. He said that you have to draw on human experiences to be a real actor or filmmaker. I hope that my life experiences and combat action will make for an interesting book or movie someday.

# WRITING

I am not an OXFORD-trained literate by any means. My book, **COMBAT JOURNAL**, will be about how and what I feel going through this life experience. I am still developing my nonfiction writing techniques as we speak. My writing background has been mainly writing dialogue for the screen or school newspapers. The *American History, A Veteran's Perspective* series of books are my first efforts into the literary publishing world. Commerciality is the furthest thing from my mind. If I do not land a book deal, I will then publish my memoirs by myself. Eventually, I hope to produce my story into a motion picture. These aren't grandiose dreams, it is just my world, and I see them as quite attainable. I will base the motion picture on my real-life experiences in real-world combat operations in Iraq through 2004 and into 2005. I guess that I feel that I have a story to tell. Anyway, folks, these are my dreams. You have to have dreams in your life.

At the time of our deployment, I was decisively engaged in a master's degree program in American History. Unfortunately, I had to put those academic pursuits on hold until after we returned home.

In addition to my duties as Battalion Executive Officer and writing the book about my adventures in Iraq, I am putting together a DVD scrapbook for the battalion.

# FAMILY

I married the most beautiful girl on the Temple University campus, Lynette, formerly of West Chester, PA. Lynette was a professional ballet-jazz-tap dancer while attending Temple. We had several classes together, started dating, and the rest is history. Lynette has since entered the teaching profession and has earned her Master's Degree in Education.

Lynette, John, John Jr., and Kristina celebrate July 4th, 2005.

# MY BEST FRIEND

My best friend was my Father. Unfortunately, my father passed away on May 25, 2003, just one year ago. Yes, this has been quite a year for my family, as we also lost my Mother just two months before Dad died. If you haven't lived through the experience of losing a parent, my dear friends, you owe it to yourself to start preparing now, as it can be a rough ride. My Father was truly my best friend. To lose your Father and your best friend all in one day was quite life-altering. Man, was that a difficult experience! I miss that old dude!

Following combat duty in World War II, my father, John F. McBrearty, utilized the GI Bill to obtain both a Bachelor and Master's Degree from Penn State University. He also received a Doctor of Philosophy Degree in Psychology from the University of Texas at Austin. Those achievements propelled Dr. McBrearty to have a successful career as a clinical psychologist and university professor at both Purdue and Temple Universities. (The photo is taken from American History, A Veteran's Perspective, Volume I, Essays, Reflections, and Reviews.)

# SISTER

I only have one sister, and she has chosen not to support me in the war efforts of our country. Too bad, all I know is that if our founding fathers did not support one another at the time of our Revolution, our country would have never happened. Enough said on this subject. I think that her actions are tragic, and I would not wish this situation upon my worst enemies. (Did I tell you that somebody shot at me this week, I guess *they* would be considered a real adversary?) Put that into perspective when you get into your next argument, particularly with your own blood relative, like a sister. It saddens me not to be supported in the war effort by a family member, but I deal with it. Despite her convictions, I still love her. To have the freedom to disagree without fear of persecution, what a wonderful country we live in. Enough with my problems.

# MUSIC

*Linkin Park* does it for me; I love their music. I guess it is the rocker in me at heart; I have always loved to rock and always will. You may or may not remember me playing the trumpet and bass guitar during High School in several rock bands? Here in Iraq, there are only Arabic-speaking radio stations, so we have to listen to CDs, MP3s, and of course, iPods for our music. I spend quite a bit of time listening to *Linkin Park*, *Alice in Chains*, *Led Zeppelin*, and the *Rolling Stones* (old-school rocker or what?)

John playing Bass Guitar in a High School rock band, 1977-78

# 9-11

Folks, 9-11 is our Pearl Harbor. What I am doing is a direct result of 9-11. Trust me, my life changed dramatically from that date. I worked 7 days a week for a year following that tragic day. The culmination for our family, obviously, is this deployment. The deployment is in excess of eighteen months in length, with a high likelihood of an extension. When I left home, my son, John Jr., was in diapers, and my daughter Kristina was leaving High School and starting her first year of college as a pre-med student. When I get back, Kristina will be a junior in college, and John Jr. will be ready for preschool. I guess that is my commitment and sacrifice to our country and all of you; I missed out on those precious years (not to mention one heck of a 25th High School Reunion this year!) Luckily, my wife Lynette, who is made of bedrock, is holding things together quite well. I am one of the lucky ones over here. (*If all goes as planned, I will be home by late May '05 and will be visiting family in Pennsylvania in July '05.*)

# HOBBIES

Golf, weights, and more golf. Writing my **COMBAT JOURNAL**.

# LIFE IN IRAQ

This is the way it is for a soldier in combat. You have to prepare for the worst. We buried a fellow Soldier from our Camp this week, as well as another Soldier from our brigade. I have attended TOO many memorial services! The price of freedom has come with the color of blood, as it has since the conception of our beloved country. I hope the American people will not forget about our sacrifices for the cause of democracy and freedom.

# IN SUMMARY

Combat duty is tough, but we do not have it that bad. No matter how bad things get, I know that there are Soldiers and Marines over here that have it far worse than us. The frequency of enemy attacks is lessening, and the Iraqi people as a whole are taking a liking to us. The Iraqis appreciate our humanitarian efforts that we have accomplished. Unfortunately, those efforts don't often make the front-page news.

# MORAL OF THE STORY

The moral of the story is to live each and every moment of your life like it could be your last. Tell your loved ones that you, in fact, love them. Spend more time with your family. Look at yourself in the mirror and ask yourself the hard questions. None of us is invincible, and we will all die at some point. How do you want to be remembered by family and friends? What I do know is that when you go out of this world, all you have is your family and maybe a few good FRIENDS. Make the most of that and cherish your loved ones.

God bless,

*And remember, I wish peace, love, and happiness to everyone.*
(from Greystones Yearbook, 1978)

I hope to see some of you in July 2005!

Your friend,

John J. McBrearty

Major John J. McBrearty
Executive Officer
Armor Battalion
Central-South Region, Iraq

MAJ John McBrearty June 11, 2004, in Iraq

# About the Author

Lt. Colonel John J. McBrearty (32 years of military service): John J. McBrearty entered the military in 1979 as a private. He had the unique distinction of serving in both the United States Marine Corps and later in the United States Army. Following battalion command, John J. McBrearty's 32-year military career culminated in his position as the brigade executive officer, Army National Guard. His career spanned the globe with operations in Iraq, Kuwait, Japan, Australia, Mexico, and Thailand. His actions and over 32 years of military duty are in keeping with the finest traditions of military service, and he was recognized by President Barak Obama.

In 2016 John McBrearty retired as a Lieutenant Colonel.

John J. McBrearty, a member of Phi Beta Kappa, is a *magna cum laude* graduate of the Valley Forge Military Academy and College as well as Temple University. He also holds a master's degree in American history from the American Public University and served as an assistant professor of Military Science at California State University, San Bernardino and Claremont McKenna College. His unique multi-service career, increasingly significant military assignments, and combat action give him insight into the importance of American history and freedom.

John J. McBrearty is author to *American History, a Veteran's Perspective, Volume I,* **ESSAYS, REFLECTIONS, AND REVIEWS**," which is available at both Amazon and Barnes & Noble. John J. McBrearty's other works have been published or featured in Sports Illustrated, Golf Week, Stars and Stripes, Callaway Magazine, Golf Digest, Grizzly Magazine, the Los Angeles Times, the Orange County Register, Main Line Times, News of Delaware County, Daily Bulletin, San Bernardino Sun, Press Enterprise, and others.

Having joined the ranks of the "retired," John is active with several Veterans Affairs support groups. He is a golf instructor and an avid player. John currently lives with his family in Southern California. He is currently completing his autobiographical combat story, **"COMBAT JOURNAL,** *American History, A Veteran's Perspective, Volumes III & IV."*

Lt. Colonel John J. McBrearty shares some similarities with the following individuals:

J. D. Salinger ("Catcher in the Rye" author).

Normal Schwarzkopf (General, U.S. Army, Commander of United States Central Command and led all coalition forces in the Gulf War "Desert Storm").

H. R. McMaster (Lieutenant General, U.S. Army, former National Security Advisor to President Donald J. Trump).

All of these individuals, as well as LTC John J. McBrearty, are graduates of Valley Forge Military Academy and College and published authors.

Thank you very much for reading my book.

Please feel free to post your thoughts in a review on Amazon

https://www.amazon.com/stores/John-J.-McBrearty/author/B0BNFDG3VF?

Made in the USA
Columbia, SC
08 July 2024

38291687R00067